Dear Reader,

Thank you for choosing to buy or read Ellie's Day at the Zoo for your child or children. This book was written with love, care, and a purpose—to encourage early childhood education and inspire young learners, ages 2-5, to explore the vibrant world around them.

Published in the USA in 2025, this story is a celebration of curiosity, imagination, and the joy of learning. It is my hope that through Ellie's adventures, your child not only discovers the magic of learning but also realizes that learning opportunities are everywhere, waiting to be embraced.

Ellie's series of storybooks proudly support the First Amendment and the freedom to read, celebrating the diverse experiences that make our world so rich. By reading this book, you are nurturing a love for learning and helping to lay the foundation for a lifetime of exploration and discovery.

Thank you for making this journey with Ellie and for believing in the power of early education. Your support of this book's mission means the world.

Warm regards,
Gregory Elliotte
Author of Ellie's Day at the Zoo

It was a warm sunny morning, and Ellie woke up extra early. Today was a special day. He was going to the zoo with his family!

"Get ready, Ellie!" called his mom. Ellie quickly put on his glasses, his favorite red t-shirt, blue jeans, and red-and-white sneakers. He grabbed his backpack and headed downstairs ready for the adventure.

When they arrived at the zoo, Ellie's eyes got very wide with excitement.

First, Ellie and his family visited the bear exhibit. The big brown bear was standing near a little pond, while a smaller bear was playfully rolling in the grass.

Ellie pretended to be a bear, growling and showing his claws towards the other bears, but the big bear did not like that very much.

Next, Ellie visited the lion's cave. Some lions were resting, and another was roaring loudly. Ellie loved the sound of the lion's loud roar, he loved the sound so much he tried it himself, he took a deep breath and Roooaaar'd as loud as he could.

Ellie's next stop was the monkeys. The monkeys were swinging from vines and chattering loudly.

Ellie then asked, "can we see the elephants please? When Ellie got to the elephant's exhibit, he noticed elephants splashing water with their trunks at each other.

Ellie's next stop was the tigers and cheetahs
"WOW, the tiger has stripes, and the cheetah has spots!" Ellie said.
Ellie seen the cheetahs running very fast. Ellie started to pretend to run fast like a cheetah. "Zoom, zoom, zoom!

In the owl exhibit, Ellie whispered, "Hoo, Hoo!" Ellie pretended to be an owl, turning his head side to side and soaring around with his arms back and forth.

As the sun began to set, Ellie looked at his family and smiled.
"This was the best day ever!" he said.

Ellie's fun day at the zoo was over, but he couldn't wait for his next adventure.

ABOUT THE AUTHOR

Gregory Elliotte, the visionary author behind the beloved Ellie's Story Book Learning Adventures!

Gregory created the Ellie series with a heartfelt mission: to ignite curiosity, imagination, and a passion for learning in young children. Aimed at ages 2-6, these vibrant, colorful, and captivating books make education enjoyable while teaching essential early childhood concepts like colors, animals, and community.

Through relatable adventures and vibrant illustrations, Gregory introduces readers to Ellie, a curious and cheerful young boy who finds delight in learning through everyday experiences. Each story is designed to inspire creativity and establish foundational skills, making it an ideal series to begin your child's reading adventure!

Why Choose the Ellie Series? It promotes and encourages early literacy, inspires creativity, and imagination. Also, it builds confidence and connection. It is tailored for young learners.

Gregory Elliotte believes that every child deserves the chance to see the world through a lens of wonder—and books are the perfect place to start! Join Ellie on his adventures and provide your little ones with the gift of lifelong learning!

Ellie's Day at the Zoo

Written By Gregory Elliotte

Published by Jazzy Kitty Publications

Wilmington, Delaware

877.782.5550 - http://www.jazzykittypublications.com

anelda@jazzykittypublications.com

Copyright © 2025 Gregory Elliotte

ISBN 978-1-965381-19-9

All rights are explicitly reserved worldwide. This book is protected under the copyright laws of the United States of America. This book may not be copied or reprinted for commercial profit or net income. The purpose of short quotations or occasional page copying for personal or group study is permitted and promoted. Permission to copy will be freely granted upon request for Worldwide Distribution, printed and published in the United States of America. Created Jazzy Kitty Greetings Marketing & Publishing, LLC dba Jazzy Kitty Publications, is utilizing Microsoft Publishing, Photoshop, and BookCoverly Software.

www.ingramcontent.com/pod-product-compliance
Lightning Source LLC
Chambersburg PA
CBHW041404010526
44107CB00015B/1072